323.143

# MALCOLM X

DAVID DOWNING

Heinemann
LIBRARY

# www.heinemann.co.uk/library

Visit our website to find out more information about **Heinemann Library** books.

To order:
 Phone 44 (0) 1865 888066
 Send a fax to 44 (0) 1865 314091
Visit the Heinemann Bookshop at www.heinemann.co.uk/library to browse our
catalogue and order online.

First published in Great Britain by Heinemann Library,
Halley Court, Jordan Hill, Oxford OX2 8EJ,
part of Harcourt Education.
Heinemann is a registered trademark of Harcourt Education Ltd.

OXFORD MELBOURNE AUCKLAND
JOHANNESBURG BLANTYRE GABORONE
IBADAN PORTSMOUTH (NH) USA
CHICAGO

Designed by AMR
Originated by Dot Gradations Ltd
Printed and bound in China by South China Printing Company

ISBN 0 431 13866 4
07 06 05 04 03
10 9 8 7 6 5 4 3 2 1

**British Library Cataloguing in Publication Data**
Downing, David
  Malcolm X. – (Leading lives)
  1.X, Malcolm, 1925–1965 2.African American civil rights
  workers – Biography – Juvenile literature
  3.United States –
  Politics and government – 20th century – Juvenile
  literature 4.United States – History – 20th century –
  Juvenile literature
  I.Title
  323'.1'196'073'092

**Acknowledgements**
The publishers would like to thank the following for permission to reproduce photographs:
Associated Press pp. 16, 36, 38, 44, 48, 53; Camera Press pp. 45, 50; Capital Area District Library p. 15; Corbis pp. 5, 21, 31, 39, 41; Culver Pictures p. 19, Hulton Archive pp. 7, 24, 29, 42; Magnum p. 55 (Eve Arnold); Picture Quest p. 22 (Peter Vandermark/Stock Boston Inc.); Popperfoto pp. 6, 12, 27, 32, 37, 51.

Cover photograph reproduced with permission of Hulton Archive.

Every effort has been made to contact copyright holders of any material reproduced in this book. Any omissions will be rectified in subsequent printings if notice is given to the publishers.

Our thanks to Christopher Gibb for his comments in the preparation of this book.

# Contents

Any words appearing in the text in bold, **like this**, are explained in the Glossary.

# 1 Incident in Harlem

The year is 1957. It is a bright spring day in Harlem, the district of New York City which is home to a million **African Americans**. A fight starts on the sidewalk, and the police arrive to break it up. They order the spectators to move on, but two smartly dressed young men refuse. The police attack one of these men, Hinton Johnson, viciously clubbing him around the head. With blood pouring from wounds, he is bundled into a car and driven off to the 28th Precinct police station. The other man hurries off in search of a payphone.

The man who takes his call has the strange name of Malcolm X. He is the **minister** of the local temple of the **Nation of Islam**. The **Muslims**, as followers of the Nation are called, preach that the white man is the devil, and that African Americans need to separate themselves from his evil influence. Malcolm X, a thin African American with light brown skin and reddish hair, is 32 years old and comes from the **Midwest** region of the USA. He has become convinced of the Nation's teachings while serving a prison sentence for armed burglary. He will go on to become one of the most influential African Americans of the late 20th century.

He quickly gathers together 50 Muslims and hurries down to the police station where Hinton Johnson is being held. The Muslims line up outside on 123rd Street with their arms folded across their chests; their short haircuts, dark glasses, suits and unsmiling faces make them look both dignified and determined. Malcolm goes inside and demands to see the prisoner.

The desk sergeant first denies that Johnson is there, and then refuses to allow Malcolm to see him. But the unspoken threat of the Muslims outside, now reinforced by a growing crowd, convinces him to change his mind. Malcolm is taken in to see Johnson, and demands that he be taken to hospital.

The police order an ambulance; the Muslims follow it up Lenox Avenue to the hospital. Again they gather in the street, and this time the police demand that they leave. Malcolm refuses: they are breaking no laws, he says, and once again the police back down. Malcolm orders the Muslims back to the temple only when a messenger emerges from the hospital to confirm that Johnson is receiving treatment.

Next day the incident makes the national newspapers. African Americans have stood up to the police and won! Across Harlem there is a feeling that something has changed, and everyone is talking about the Muslims and Malcolm X.

▲ *Lenox Avenue in Harlem in the 1950s, where Malcolm X first came to prominence after standing up to authority on behalf of African Americans.*

# Early years

On Christmas Eve 1924, a bunch of hooded **Ku Klux Klansmen** holding flaming torches surrounded a small house on the outskirts of Omaha, Nebraska. Their leader shouted that the owner of the house, a dangerously outspoken **African American** (American descendant of African slaves) named Earl Little, should come out. It is not clear whether they intended to hurt him or to kill him, but fortunately for Earl he was not at home. His pregnant wife, Louise, came to the door and told the hooded men. They made threats, smashed windows, and rode off into the night.

Five months later, on 19 May 1925, Earl's wife Louise gave birth to the child she was carrying, a third son. He had his mother's light skin, eyes that were an unusual mix of brown, blue and green, and light hair that would darken to a reddish-brown. They named him Malcolm.

▲ Members of the racist society Ku Klux Klan, in their hooded outfits designed to instil fear in African Americans.

## Earl and Louise

Earl and Louise had married in 1919 after meeting in Montreal, Canada. Louise, who was Earl's second wife, grew up on the West Indian island of Grenada. Her father, whom she never met, had been white, and Louise, with her pale skin, straight black hair and British accent, was often taken for a white woman in the USA.

Earl Little grew up in Georgia, southern USA, where he married young and had three children. This marriage broke up, and Earl moved north, leaving his family behind. Three of his brothers had been murdered by white men before he left Georgia, and not surprisingly Earl listened to anyone who had a plan for improving the conditions under which African Americans lived. In Philadelphia, where he and Louise first settled after marrying, he heard Marcus Garvey speak (see 'Key People', page 58). Greatly impressed, he joined Garvey's organization – the Universal Negro Improvement Association (UNIA) – and for the rest of his life devoted himself to spreading Garvey's ideas.

In Omaha, where Malcolm was born, his father was head of the local UNIA chapter, and Earl used to take his third son with him to meetings. It was here that the future Malcolm X, then only four years old, first heard Garvey's basic message: in the face of white **oppression** African Americans had no choice but to unite and organize themselves.

## A fire in the night

Malcolm was a keen reader from a very early age, and clearly an intelligent child. He, Philbert and Reginald – the two brothers immediately above and below him – spent most of their time together, either fighting each other or taking on the rest of the world as a threesome. The older children, Hilda and Wilfred, were already at school, and new arrivals – Yvonne, Wesley and Robert – appeared at regular intervals. Home life was strict: Earl beat the children if they broke his rules. There was also a constant threat of violence from outside. White **racists** targeted Earl because of his outspoken beliefs, and the family was frequently forced to move to avoid trouble. In 1929 they bought a house in Lansing, Michigan, but soon a local racist group called the Black Legion started making threats.

The estate agent had sold Louise the house thinking she was white, but when he discovered the family was African American, he unearthed a document saying the house should not have been sold to non-whites. The Littles were told to move out, with no offer of a refund.

A week before they were to move, men came in the night and set fire to the house. The family only just managed to escape the flames, and Earl fired off a couple of shots from his shotgun at the men responsible as they ran away. Fire fighters arrived, but showed little interest in putting out the fire. The police, when they came, were more interested in Earl shooting his gun than in who had started the fire.

▲ Marcus Garvey, the founder and leader of the Universal Negro Improvement Association, of which Malcolm's father Earl Little was an active member.

## Young gardener

Deprived of their home, the family lived in temporary lodgings while Earl built them a new house outside Lansing. This four-roomed house, according to Malcolm, was 'where I really begin to remember things … where I started to grow up.' They kept chickens and turkeys and grew a few vegetables to supplement Earl's uncertain income as a labourer. He continued with his preaching and there was no let-up in the threats to his life.

### Early lesson

*'I would cry out and make a fuss until I got what I wanted. I remember well how my mother asked me why I couldn't be a nice boy like Wilfred; but I would think to myself that Wilfred, for being so nice and quiet, often stayed hungry. So early in life, I learned that if you want something, you had better make some noise.'*

(From *The Autobiography of Malcolm X*)

Malcolm had his own little plot in the garden. He especially liked to grow peas for his family. 'I would patrol the rows on my hands and knees for any worms and bugs,' he wrote later, 'and sometimes when I had everything straight and clean for my things to grow, I would lie down on my back between two rows, and I would gaze up in the blue sky at the clouds moving and think all kinds of things.'

In 1930, aged five years, he started at Pleasant Grove School, setting off each morning with Hilda, Wilfred and Philbert. The Littles were the only African Americans who went there and were called 'nigger', 'darkie' or 'Rastus' by the white children. 'They didn't think of it as an insult,' Malcolm wrote. 'It was just the way they thought about us.'

## A suspicious death

One evening in 1931, Earl failed to come home after he stormed out during an argument with Louise. That night Malcolm and the other children were woken by her screams of anguish – the police had come to take her to the hospital. Earl had been found dead by the tram tracks in Lansing, his skull crushed and his body almost cut in half.

The newspapers said it was an accident, but one of the two companies Earl had bought **life insurance** from said it was suicide, and refused to pay up. Most people in the African American community thought white racists had killed him and placed his body on the tracks to make it look like an accident.

## A brief history of African Americans

The first African **slaves** were brought to the Americas in 1518. Over the next three centuries some fifteen million African men, women and children were landed in what is now known as the USA, but many more died during the Atlantic crossings. Slaves were worked to the limits of their strength, badly fed and housed. They had no legal rights. Families were often split up and women were abused by their white masters.

After the USA won independence from Great Britain in 1776, the trade in slaves was abolished but slavery continued in **the South**. Pressure from northern states eventually resulted in the defeat of the South in the American Civil War (1861–65). Slaves were then freed and African Americans were officially guaranteed equal rights.

However, in the defeated South, African Americans' rights were reduced until they were treated like slaves by many white people. The first major African American organization to fight against this was the NAACP (National Association for the Advancement of Coloured People), founded in 1909, which said that discrimination should be fought in the law courts rather than on the streets. The second, Marcus Garvey's UNIA, founded in 1914, was more radical: Garvey wanted African Americans to develop communities independent of white society.

Despite the growth of such movements, there was little improvement for most African Americans. Although African American culture blossomed – particularly in jazz music and literature – the **Great Depression** of the 1930s hit African Americans harder than most poor white people.

In World War II, African Americans still mostly fought in **segregated** units, separated from all-white units. But fighting in a global war against German and Japanese racism made it harder to justify white American racism to the watching world. Finally, in December 1955, the Montgomery Bus Boycott was the first in a series of direct challenges to white-dominated authorities. Almost a century after slaves were freed, race relations shot to the top of the American political agenda once more.

# Growing up

By his seventh birthday, Malcolm Little had already lost his father and seen his home burnt down around him, but his family's troubles were far from over. Raising eight children is an expensive business, and the money from Earl's **life insurance** policy soon disappeared.

Louise took jobs cleaning and sewing for white people. Her employers often assumed she was white herself, and on at least one occasion she was fired when they discovered she was an **African American**. The oldest son, Wilfred, left school and looked for work, but America was now in the grip of the **Great Depression**. Jobs were both hard to find and poorly paid. Malcolm and Philbert did their bit, fishing for the family supper and trapping rabbits, which they sold to white neighbours.

## Welfare

Louise made meals with day-old bread and whatever wild vegetables she could find growing. Often there was only cornmeal mush or boiled dandelion greens, and at school the children were taunted for eating 'fried grass'. They were often hungry.

◀ Long queues formed for jobs, food and accommodation during the Great Depression of the 1930s.

Conquering her pride, Louise applied for **welfare**. The
monthly cheque was small, and the family continued to live in
poverty, but at least they did not starve. Unfortunately, the
welfare people thought these payments entitled them to make
frequent visits and ask insulting questions, such as why
Malcolm's skin was so much lighter than that of his brothers
and sisters. Louise was upset by these intrusions, but when
she objected, the welfare people told her she was being
difficult and ungrateful. To young Malcolm it seemed as if they
were more interested in proving Louise was a bad mother
than in helping the family.

## Losing a mother

In 1936, Louise met a man who liked her, and for a year or so
it looked like the family might have a new father. But the man,
perhaps put off by the thought of eight young mouths to feed,
suddenly stopped coming around, and Louise started acting
strangely. She would stare into space for hours on end, or
walk around talking to herself. She no longer seemed to
notice her increasingly terrified children. 'We watched our
anchor giving way,' Malcolm wrote later.

The welfare workers found **foster homes** for the children.
Malcolm was the first to go, moving in with another local
family, the Gohannases. He ate better and enjoyed the
company of the Gohannases' son Big Boy, but missed his
own family.

In January 1939, Louise suffered a complete mental
breakdown and was sent away to the State Mental Hospital in
Kalamazoo. Wilfred and Hilda stayed on in the family home
but the other children were all fostered out to local homes.
The family had been broken up.

## Trying to fit in

Malcolm was deeply upset, and his behaviour at his new school worsened. Expelled for putting a drawing pin on his teacher's chair, he was told that he would be going to **reform school**. First he was sent to a **juvenile detention home**, where he was given a room of his own for the first time in his life. The adults who ran the home liked him, and decided to enrol him in the local school rather than send him on to the reform school.

As he was the only African American in his year, Malcolm had to make an effort to fit in – he was trying, as he later said, to be white. He was a bright pupil who enjoyed studying and sports like basketball and football, and he was popular enough to be voted Class President. Malcolm tried to tell himself that the constant racial insults were not really meant; he tried to ignore the fact that his history teacher passed over the history of African Americans with a few words and a cheap joke. At school dances he accepted the fact that he would not do any dancing because all the girls were white.

## History lesson

'We came to the textbook section on Negro history. It was exactly one paragraph long. Mr Williams [Malcolm's teacher] laughed through it practically in a single breath, reading aloud how the Negroes had been slaves and then were freed, and how they were usually lazy and dumb and shiftless.'

(From *The Autobiography of Malcolm X*)

◀ *Lansing, Michigan in the late 1930s, when Malcolm was growing up there.*

There was only so much humiliation he could take. Asked by one of his favourite teachers what he intended to do with his life, he suggested a career in law. The teacher looked surprised. 'You've got to be realistic about being a nigger,' he told Malcolm. 'A lawyer – that's no realistic goal for a nigger. You need to think about something you can be. You're good with your hands … Why don't you plan on carpentry?'

Many of Malcolm's white classmates were less bright than he was, but they were encouraged to choose whatever career attracted them. 'It was then that I began to change – inside,' he wrote in his autobiography.

In the spring of 1940, Malcolm's older half-sister Ella – one of the three children from Earl Little's first marriage – invited him to spend the summer with her in the east coast city of Boston. He had never seen such a big and busy city before, and found it thrilling. The experience of walking through Roxbury district – where most of Boston's **African Americans** lived – was a real eye-opener. Here, African Americans seemed to be doing what Garvey and his father had said they should: they were living their own lives, independently of whites.

▲ *The house in Roxbury, Boston, where Malcolm lived with his half-sister Ella.*

## Boston

Back home in Lansing, Malcolm wrote regularly to Ella, asking if he could live with her on a permanent basis. Early in 1941, she finally agreed. Ella told him to look around for a while, to get to know the city, before he looked for jobs. She hoped he would find work near home, in the more respectable part of Roxbury where they lived, but Malcolm had other ideas. He was drawn to the more exciting world of Lower Roxbury, a world of bars and pool halls, of musicians and thieves and hustlers.

He met another youth from Lansing named Shorty, who taught him how to look 'cool': how to **conk**, or straighten his hair by applying a burning mixture of ingredients, and what clothes to buy. Soon Malcolm was the proud owner of a sky blue 'zoot suit' with its fashionably baggy-kneed, thin-ankled trousers.

### First 'conk'

*'This was my first really big step toward self-degradation: when I endured all of that pain, literally burning my flesh to have it look like a white man's hair. I had joined that multitude of Negro men and women in America who are brainwashed into believing that the black people are "inferior" – and white people "superior" – that they will even violate and mutilate their God-created bodies to try to look "pretty" by white standards.'*
(From *The Autobiography of Malcolm X*)

Shorty got Malcolm a job working as a shoeshine boy at the famous Roseland State Ballroom. Shining shoes was only part of the job – Malcolm was soon supplying his customers with whatever they wanted, anything from drugs to women. These were illegal activities, but commonplace in Lower Roxbury. Malcolm loved listening and dancing to the great jazz orchestras – led by people like Duke Ellington and Count Basie – that played at the Ballroom. He even left his job as a shoeshine because it took up time he could have spent dancing!

## Harlem

Ella found him another job, working in a local drugstore. Here he met Laura, who was exactly the sort of nice young African American woman that Ella wanted him to meet. They went out together a couple of times, but then Malcolm rejected her in favour of a white woman named Bea.

Ella, hoping to get him away from Bea, who she thought would bring trouble for Malcolm, found him a job working on the railroad from Boston to New York. He started off loading goods in the yards, and eventually took over as the train's 'sandwich man', threading his way through the moving carriages of the 'Yankee Clipper' with his shoulder-strap box of sandwiches. He acted the clown to get good tips, but frequently went too far in his jokey abuse of the customers. There were regular complaints and eventually he was fired.

## Fighting back

'A big, beefy, red-faced **cracker** soldier got up in front of me, so drunk he was weaving, and announced loud enough that everybody in the car [railway carriage] could hear him, "I'm going to fight you, nigger". I remember the tension. I laughed and told him, "Sure, I'll fight, but you've got too many clothes on". He had a big Army overcoat. He took that off, and I kept laughing and said he still had on too many. I was able to keep that cracker stripping off clothes until he stood there drunk with nothing on from his pants up, and the whole car was laughing at him, and some other soldiers got him out of the way. ... I never would forget that – that I couldn't have whipped that white man as badly with a club as I had with my mind.'

(From *The Autobiography of Malcolm X*)

Between trips, Malcolm had explored New York's Harlem district, home to the largest urban African American population in the USA. He fell in love with the atmosphere and the excitement, and after losing his railroad job he moved there, renting a room on 126th Street. Early in the summer of 1942, he got a job as a waiter at Smalls Paradise Bar, one of Harlem's most famous gathering places. Celebrities from all walks of life – both legal and illegal – could be found sitting over a drink in Smalls.

▲ *Smalls Paradise Bar in the 1940s. Malcolm loved working here, and began his career as a small-time criminal through the contacts he made among the customers.*

Malcolm was in 'seventh heaven seven times over.' He used to arrive an hour early for work so that he could talk to the customers, men like the legendary pickpocket Fewclothes and the famous **cat-burglar** Jumpstead. He learned about the **numbers game**, about **confidence tricks** and drug dealing, and about how to sell stolen goods. He learned about people, and what made them tick. His many new friends, not quite sure where Lansing was, called him 'Detroit Red' after his reddish hair.

## Going bad

Although he occasionally visited his brothers and sisters in Lansing, his own life now seemed so different from theirs. In early 1943, he lost his job at Small's, and for the next three years lived as a criminal. He worked as a drug dealer, first in Harlem and then up and down the East Coast, supplying touring bands of musicians. Later that year he committed a string of armed robberies in partnership with a man named Sammy, and narrowly escaped capture on several occasions. He took a lot of drugs and always carried a gun.

The police were watching Malcolm's every move and he had a growing number of enemies in the underworld. It seemed only a matter of time before someone caught up with him, and late in 1945 he became involved in a dispute with a well-known criminal named West Indian Archie. Just in time, he headed back to Boston.

Ella was shocked at how different he was, but Malcolm showed no sign of wanting to change his ways. He formed a burglary gang with Bea, her sister, his old friend Shorty and another African American named Rudy. The two women would bluff their way into houses to check out what was worth stealing, and later two of the men would break in while the other waited in the car. They conducted a string of successful robberies over Christmas 1945, but then their luck ran out. Malcolm had left a stolen watch with a jeweller for repair, and when he returned to pick it up the police were waiting for him.

The two women were put on **probation**, but Malcolm and Shorty were sentenced to eight to ten years in prison, more than double the usual sentence for such crimes. Most observers thought that the judge was also punishing them for having relationships with white women.

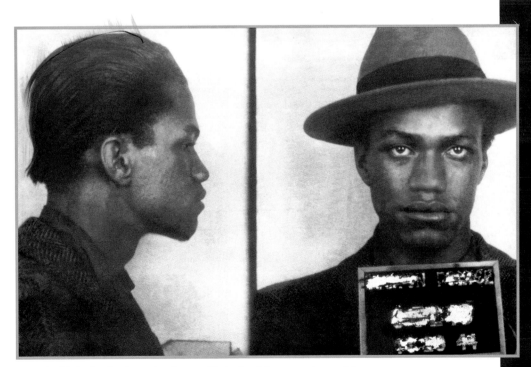

▲ *Malcolm Little – the future Malcolm X – complete with conked hair, as photographed by the Massachusetts State Police.*

# Prison

The conditions in Boston's Charlestown Prison were terrible. The cells were small, overcrowded and dirty, with one bucket for a toilet and another for washing in. The guards were abusive and often vicious. For Malcolm, deprived of both freedom and drugs, it was like a nightmare come true. Bitter and angry, he lashed out at guards and fellow prisoners alike, earning the nickname 'Satan'. He was frequently sent to the solitary punishment cells, where he would 'pace for hours like a caged leopard, viciously cursing aloud to myself.'

▲ The red brick apartment buildings and Bunker Hill monument in Charlestown, the area of Boston where Malcolm spent his first few years of imprisonment for robbery.

Gradually he calmed down. A fellow prisoner named Bimbi convinced him to make use of his time inside, perhaps by taking one of the **correspondence courses** which the prison offered. At around the same time, his sister Hilda wrote suggesting he should try to improve his writing, as she had barely been able to read his last postcard.

Malcolm took their advice, but also became more involved with the illegal side of prison life, running flourishing businesses selling cigarettes and gambling. His wild anger had gone, but he was still a hustler.

## The Nation of Islam

After almost two years in Charlestown he was transferred to a prison in Concord, Massachusetts. Here he received two interesting letters from his brothers. Reginald told Malcolm to give up cigarettes and eating pork, and Philbert wrote telling him that he had joined something called the **Nation of Islam**, which represented 'the natural religion of the black man'. Malcolm did not make any connection between the two letters at first, but gradually became aware that all his older siblings – Wilfred, Hilda, Philbert and Reginald – had joined the Nation and now called themselves '**Muslims**'. Why had it attracted so many members of his family?

Late in 1948, and mostly thanks to Ella, he was transferred again, this time to the Norfolk Prison Colony. Here there were flushing toilets and single rooms with doors rather than bars. The library was enormous, the visiting rules less strict.

One of Malcolm's first visitors was Reginald. He had been sent by the family to convince Malcolm that his future lay with the Nation of Islam and its leader Elijah Muhammad. God was a man, Reginald told him. His real name was '**Allah**'. And the devil was also a man – the white man.

Over the next few days Malcolm thought about this, about all the white men he had ever known: the hooded men who had hounded and probably killed his father; the ones in suits who called his mother crazy and took her away; the teacher who told him to be 'realistic' about a career ... The list went on and on, right down to the judge who had sentenced him. At this point in his life Malcolm had met none of the many white Americans who hated **racism**, and who were committed to fighting it. What reasons had he for thinking that the Nation of Islam was wrong?

## Myths and truths

Slowly Malcolm formed a complete picture of the Nation of Islam's teachings. According to Elijah Muhammad's version of **Islam**, which differed greatly from traditional views of Islam, Africans were descendants of the 'Original' people. These had been highly advanced beings, in tune with nature and capable of communicating with another race on Mars.

◀ *Elijah Muhammad, leader of the Nation of Islam.*

## The Nation of Islam

The Nation of Islam was founded in Detroit around 1930 by a man who called himself Wallace Fard Muhammad. It was a political religion which borrowed many beliefs and practices from true Islam, but which was also specifically designed as a set of ideas for helping African Americans to free themselves from white domination. Its followers called themselves Muslims. In 1934 Fard mysteriously disappeared, and was replaced as leader by his disciple Elijah Poole, who then took the name Elijah Muhammad.

But one of their number, an evil scientist named Yacub, had created the white race, who were destined to create hell on Earth for black people for 6000 years. Their time was now nearly up, and Elijah Muhammad was preparing **African Americans** to inherit the Earth once the white races destroyed themselves.

This was the Nation of Islam's central **myth** and like many myths it sounded rather far-fetched. Still, it fitted many of the facts as Malcolm saw them. It explained why whites behaved the way they did towards African Americans, and why Christianity offered them nothing more than a blue-eyed Jesus and a heaven after death.

Malcolm was drawn even more strongly by the political lessons of the myth. If the white man really was evil, then it made sense to declare war on him. The first step, as Reginald said, was to recognize who your enemy was.

From that, everything else followed: the pride in one's own race, the economic independence and the right to self-defence. Marcus Garvey had argued for all of these things and so had Malcolm's father.

Malcolm wrote the first of many letters to Elijah Muhammad and received the first of many replies. Soon he was a committed Muslim. His life had changed; it had discipline and direction. 'I still marvel at how swiftly my previous life's thinking pattern slid away from me, like snow from a roof,' he wrote. It was as though someone else had lived his previous life of hustling and crime.

## College behind bars

His remaining years in prison were spent in self-education. Studying awoke inside him 'some long dormant craving to be mentally alive', and he read books by the hundred, often studying deep into the night by the dim glow of the corridor light. He went through the dictionary word by word, improving his vocabulary. He read biographies, literature, **philosophy**. They confirmed what the Nation of Islam was telling him, that white history books had little to say about African Americans or the crimes that had been committed against them.

When he finally emerged from prison, aged 27, in the summer of 1952, he badly needed glasses. He was also filled with a new determination: 'I made up my mind to devote the rest of my life to telling the white man about himself – or die.'

Malcolm's first action as a free man was to steam off the smell of prison at a Turkish bath. After staying the night with Ella, he took the bus west towards Detroit, where his brother Wilfred had found him a job at the furniture store he managed. Looking out of the window as the miles rolled by, he must have noticed many ways in which the outside world had

▲ Detroit in the 1950s, where Malcolm lived after his release from prison.

changed during his six and a half years in prison. And he must have also thought about the changes that had taken place inside himself.

He moved in with Wilfred and his family, and each day he accompanied his brother to the furniture store. He was not very comfortable with the work, which often consisted of persuading people to buy things on **credit** which they could not really afford, but his new life as a **Muslim** in the **Nation of Islam** was everything he had hoped for. At home he adopted the routines of cleansing, praying and eating which were expected of Muslims, and after work he would spend much of his time at the Nation of Islam's temple in Detroit, Temple Number One. There he would listen to **Minister** Lemuel Hassan explaining the teachings of Elijah Muhammad and he would enjoy the company of his fellow Muslims. Never before had he been among such a neatly dressed, serious group of **African Americans**. Never before had he felt such pride in his people. His only sadness was the number of seats that still remained empty.

## A new life

'I had never dreamed of anything like that atmosphere among black people who had learned to be proud they were black, who had learned to love other black people instead of being jealous and suspicious. I thrilled to how we Muslim men used both hands to grasp a black brother's both hands, voicing and smiling our happiness to meet him again. The Muslim sisters, both married and single, were given an honour and respect that I'd never seen black men give to their women, and it felt wonderful to me. The salutations which we all exchanged were warm, filled with mutual respect and dignity: "Brother"... "Sister"... "Ma'am"... "Sir." Even children speaking to other children used these terms. Beautiful!'

(From *The Autobiography of Malcolm X*)

## Elijah Muhammad

Three weeks after Malcolm's arrival in Detroit, the whole congregation of Temple Number One travelled to Chicago to visit the Nation of Islam's leader Elijah Muhammad. Malcolm had not been so excited since childhood, and the experience fully lived up to his expectations. He stared at the 'sensitive, gentle, brown face' that he had seen before only in photographs, and listened intently as Elijah Muhammad addressed the meeting.

Then, to Malcolm's surprise, he heard his own name – Elijah Muhammad was asking him to stand up. He did so.

Elijah Muhammad told the audience how he and Malcolm had written to each other while Malcolm was in prison, and then reminded everyone of a story in the Bible. The devil had told God that Job was faithful only because God had protected him from temptation, Elijah Muhammad said, and if he was here now, the devil might say that Malcolm had remained faithful only because he was protected by prison walls, and that now he would return to his drugs and his criminal life. 'I believe that he is going to remain faithful,' Elijah Muhammad said.

Malcolm's belief was strengthened still further. 'I had more faith in Elijah Muhammad than I could ever have in any other man upon this earth,' he wrote later. For his part, Elijah Muhammad recognized Malcolm's commitment. Soon after the visit to Chicago, Malcolm received his 'X', the Muslim surname which he now took in place of Little. Little, after all, was simply the name that a white man had given one of his slave ancestors.

▲ A Nation of Islam meeting, around 1955.

## Fishing for converts

During the visit to Chicago Malcolm had asked Elijah Muhammad about the empty seats in Temple Number One. How should they go about filling them? 'Go after the young people,' Elijah Muhammad said. 'Once you get them the older ones will follow through shame.'

Back in Detroit Malcolm followed his advice. There were always young people hanging out on the street near the temple, young people who thought and acted much as Malcolm had in his earlier life. He went out looking for them, 'fishing for converts' as he called it, in bars and pool halls. He told them his own story, and of how he had found pride in himself and his people through the Muslims. Many scoffed, but each week a few more would end up in the temple. By the end of the year the congregation had tripled.

## Remembering slavery

*'I know you don't realize the enormity, the horrors, of the so-called Christian white man's crime ... Not even in the Bible is there such a crime! God in his wrath struck down with fire the perpetrators of lesser crimes! One hundred million of us black people! Your grandparents! Mine! Murdered by this white man. To get fifteen million of us here to make his slaves, on the way he murdered one hundred million! I wish it was possible for me to show you the sea bottom in those days – the black bodies, the blood, the bones broken by boots and clubs! The pregnant black women who were thrown overboard if they got sick. Thrown overboard to the sharks that had learned that following these slave ships was the way to grow fat!'*

(From *The Autobiography of Malcolm X*. Note that the figures used by Malcolm are his own guesses)

◀ An engraving of a slave auction. Malcolm found converts to the Nation of Islam by reminding people of the horrors of slavery.

Malcolm was becoming a good and persuasive speaker. He was clever, witty and, most important of all, quite prepared to express opinions many other African Americans also held but were afraid to express. There was no uncertainty in his message, no 'on the one hand, on the other hand'. The white man was the devil, he said, and it was time the African American acted accordingly.

He often began by reminding his audiences of their terrible history, of the horrors of the **slave trade** and **slavery**. 'Do you know why the white man really hates you?' he would ask his audience. 'It's because every time he sees your face, he sees a mirror of his crime – and his guilty conscience can't bear to face it!'

On other occasions he would offer them a bitter joke: 'We didn't land on Plymouth Rock, my brothers and sisters – Plymouth Rock landed on us!' (Plymouth Rock in Massachusetts was where the Pilgrim Fathers, famous early settlers of North America, came ashore in 1620.)

## A rising star

Malcolm's enormous talent was clear. In June 1953 he was given the full-time post of Assistant Minister at Temple Number One. Sixth months later Elijah Muhammad sent him to set up Temple Number Eleven in Boston, and to 'fish for converts' on the very streets where he had started hustling. Once this new temple was up and running he was given the task of setting up Temple Number Twelve in Philadelphia. This took him less than three months, and by June 1954 he was on his way to New York and Harlem, the heart of African America.

▶ *Philadephia in the 1950s, one of many cities where Malcolm successfully found recruits for the Nation of Islam.*

# 7 The Hate That Hate Produced

The people of Harlem were Malcolm's greatest challenge.
After giving his speeches explaining the **African American**
situation, most listeners believed what he had said. But when
he asked if they would join the **Nation of Islam**, the answer
was usually no. To be a **Muslim** you had to give up alcohol,
tobacco, drugs, sex outside marriage and gambling –
entertainments that were widespread in Harlem at that time.
The congregation of Harlem's Temple Number Seven grew, but
only slowly.

Malcolm helped set up Nation of Islam businesses – usually
restaurants and grocery stores – as part of the organization's
plan for achieving African American economic independence.
In Chicago, Elijah Muhammad was often ill, and Malcolm, now
Elijah's deputy in all but name, carried his teachings to all parts
of the country in 1955–56. At meetings he told African
American audiences to unite and take control of their
neighbourhoods, their local economy, their security and their
children's education.

In 1957, when a young African American named Hinton
Johnson was publicly beaten up by the police in Harlem,
Malcolm organized that display of Muslim power already
described in Chapter 1, a display which both stunned America
and made him a hero to many young African Americans.

## Betty

Malcolm's work left him little private time. The temple paid
his living expenses and provided a little pocket money, but any
other payments he received went straight back to the Nation
of Islam. A new car was provided for his use, but all he
actually owned were his clothes, suitcase and wristwatch.

He occasionally saw his brothers and sisters – particularly those active in the Nation of Islam – but he had not had a girlfriend since going into prison, and he told himself that he did not want one. Then, in 1956, he met Betty Sanders (soon to be Betty X) at Temple Number Seven.

For more than a year, the two just exchanged occasional words until Malcolm, much to his own surprise, realized that he really cared for her. He tried avoiding Betty, but could not stop thinking about her, and in January 1958 he called her up from a petrol station payphone and simply asked whether she would marry him. She said yes, and two days later they were married in Lansing. The Nation provided them with a house in the New York's Queens district, and eleven months later Betty gave birth to their first daughter, Attallah.

## Shocking America

In early 1959, Malcolm was confirmed as the Nation of Islam's chief spokesman, and toured Africa for three weeks as Elijah Muhammad's ambassador. He wrote regular columns for Harlem's *Amsterdam News* and, later, the *Los Angeles Herald Dispatch*; he also helped launch and run the Muslims' own newspaper, *Muhammad Speaks*. The television stations knew they could count on him to say things many people still considered outrageous, so he was rarely short of invitations to appear on discussion programmes. Seven years after leaving prison, Malcolm X was one of the most famous African Americans alive.

His fame, and that of the Muslims, was further boosted by a media event in 1959. *The Hate That Hate Produced* was a five-part television report by Mike Wallace. The Muslims had cooperated with the programme makers, and presented their views clearly.

Elijah Muhammad and Malcolm were shown denouncing the centuries-old ill-treatment of African Americans by the 'white devils', but it was the way the Muslims behaved which really shocked millions of white Americans. The Muslims did not plead for favours or demand **integration**. On the contrary, they were contemptuous of white society. The viewers were shown well-run businesses, martial arts lessons and dignified meetings. They were shown an African America that no longer wanted anything to do with white America.

The reaction was enormous. Many whites were shocked to find such hatred directed at them, and many young African Americans were inspired by the Muslims' message of angry defiance. The Nation of Islam continued to expand, from around 400 members in 1952 to around 40,000 in 1962. The meetings turned into huge rallies attended by tens of thousands, and Malcolm was always appearing on television, picking apart his enemies' arguments with a wicked smile and forcing them to accept unwelcome truths.

▶ *Malcolm holds up a copy of the Nation of Islam newspaper* Muhammad Speaks *during a rally in New York City, 1963.*

## The essence of his appeal

'What made him unfamiliar and dangerous was not his hatred for white people but his love for blacks, his apprehension [awareness] of the horror of the black condition and the reasons for it, and his determination so to work on their hearts and minds that they would be enabled to see their condition and change it themselves.'

(From an essay by African American writer James Baldwin)

# 8 By any means necessary

In 1960–63, the struggle against **racial discrimination** in the USA entered a dramatic phase. As the crisis deepened, and as the race issue occupied the centre stage of American politics, so Malcolm's fame and importance grew. At home in Queens he had reason to be joyful – two more daughters, Qubilah and Ilyasah, were born in 1960 and 1962 – but out in the world his enemies seemed to be multiplying.

## The wrong kind of friends

The political establishment in Washington DC had little liking for people who condemned it as **racist**, and who advocated a separate state for **African Americans** which would threaten the unity of the USA. In the relative calm of the early 1950s, a small organization like the **Nation of Islam** could be safely ignored, but by the end of the decade the **Muslims** and Malcolm were being taken much more seriously.

In September 1960, the Cuban revolutionary leader Fidel Castro visited New York to address the United Nations, and, as a deliberate gesture of support for African Americans, chose to stay at the Hotel Theresa in Harlem.

▶ *Fidel Castro acknowledging the cheers of the crowd on his arrival in New York in 1960. Castro and Malcolm were united in their opposition to the US government.*

At an informal meeting in the hotel, Castro and Malcolm found they had at least one thing in common – their opposition to the American government. The **FBI** were alarmed at the prospect of an alliance between African Americans and outside powers, especially communist ones. **Surveillance** on Malcolm and the Nation of Islam was increased.

## Malcolm and Martin

Malcolm's most famous disputes during this period were with fellow African Americans. These disputes arose mostly because of the differences in living conditions between **the South**, and the great cities of the North-East, **Midwest** and West. In the South, expressions of racism were still legal, and **civil rights** organizations like Martin Luther King's Southern

Christian Leadership Conference concentrated on persuading the **federal government** to overrule local racist laws. They did this by appealing to the political and Christian consciences of the leaders in Washington. They hoped by keeping their protests non-violent they would put their violently racist enemies in a bad light and so win sympathy for their cause.

◀ *Malcolm X with his daughters Qubilah (left) and Attalah at their home in Queens, New York City, 1962.*

Outside the old South, however, racial discrimination was neither openly proclaimed nor protected by laws, but it was just as real. What use was **integration** if most African Americans struggled against **economic discrimination**? How effective would non-violent protests be in situations where white men felt no pangs of conscience? African American leaders like Malcolm X reserved the right to use 'any means necessary'.

## African American population

The population of the USA in 1960 was 179 million, of which approximately 20 million (11%) were African Americans. Of these, around 9 million lived in the states of the old South. Most of the remaining 11 million lived in the cities of the industrial North-East, Midwest and California.

▶ Malcolm X addressing a rally in Harlem, New York City, in May 1963.

Through the early 1960s the southern 'moderates' and the young urban 'extremists' traded many insults. Moderates like Martin Luther King thought that extremists like Malcolm would end up hurting everyone, and that their talk of a separate state for African Americans was completely unrealistic. The extremists argued that moderate methods would never force the whites to grant real equality, and that 'turning the other cheek' – refusing to fight back – was just one more humiliation for African Americans to bear.

In August 1963 there was a huge civil rights march on Washington in which King played a significant part. This event was a good case in point, demonstrating the differences between the two men. Malcolm called it the 'Farce on Washington', because he thought that whites and over-cautious moderates had taken over and weakened what had started off as a purely African American protest. King pointed out what a memorable day it was, and how the success of the event had strengthened support for Kennedy's recently introduced Civil Rights Bill. Both were right.

## A view of Malcolm X

'Others were discussing the past or the future, or a country which may once have existed, or one which may yet be brought into existence – Malcolm was speaking of the bitter and unanswerable present.'

(From an essay by the African American writer James Baldwin)

Temperamentally, Malcolm was inclined to expect little from whites, while King expected a lot, and in public both tended to exaggerate these inclinations. Malcolm would stress how little had changed in the world, while King would concentrate on how much change was possible.

The two men only met once, in Washington DC in 1964. Despite their differences, they seem to have liked and respected each other.

## Enemy within

Malcolm's opponents in the establishment and among the more moderate African American leaders turned out to be less dangerous than his enemies inside the Nation of Islam. There were some arguments about policy – Malcolm, for example, favoured working with other groups – but the real cause of conflict was Malcolm's own celebrity status. The sons of Elijah Muhammad were particularly jealous of this. When Elijah's health grew worse, they set out to make sure Malcolm did not succeed him as the Nation of Islam's leader.

▲ Malcolm and Martin Luther King Jr. in Washington DC, January 1964. It was the only time the two most important African American politicians of their time met.

Malcolm had noticed that his name was appearing less often in *Muhammad Speaks*, but he soon had something much more serious to worry about. For years there had been rumours that Elijah Muhammad was having extra-marital affairs, and a large number of unexplained resignations from the Chicago temple finally forced Malcolm to investigate. He was horrified to find that the rumours were true, and that Elijah Muhammad had fathered children with at least three of his secretaries.

▲ *Malcolm speaking in Newark, New Jersey. Elijah Muhammad is sitting behind him.*

When confronted, Elijah Muhammad admitted the facts, but claimed the Nation's rules did not apply to him. Malcolm could not accept this reasoning. His faith in Elijah Muhammad had suffered a huge blow, and Elijah, knowing he had lost Malcolm's unquestioning support, waited for an opportunity to weaken the younger man's position and popularity.

It came later that year. When President Kennedy was assassinated in November, Nation of Islam **ministers** were ordered not to comment, but Malcolm, asked a direct question by a member of an audience, said that he thought 'the chickens were coming home to roost'. He meant that America's climate of hatred and violence had finally reached right to the top of American society, but many people thought he was saying that Kennedy had brought his death upon himself, and were angry with Malcolm for making such a suggestion. Elijah Muhammad immediately ordered Malcolm not to speak in public for 90 days as a punishment.

Malcolm accepted that he had made a mistake, but it soon became clear to him that Elijah Muhammad and his sons were mounting a campaign to discredit him with other Muslims. A few weeks later he was told by loyal members of Temple Number Seven that someone at Nation of Islam headquarters in Chicago had ordered his murder. This was the moment, he said, of his 'psychological divorce' from the Nation of Islam. Early in March 1964, Malcolm announced that he was parting company with the organization that had been his whole life for more than a decade.

# 9

# A shift of emphasis

Malcolm was still committed to fighting for his fellow **African Americans**, but how was he to do that outside the **Nation of Islam**? He decided to set up a rival movement, one that would really live up to its principles. On 16 March 1964 he founded **Muslim** Mosque, Inc. Many of his former colleagues at Temple Number Seven left the Nation of Islam to join him in this new organization.

For many years Malcolm had wanted to do what all true Muslims hoped to do at least once in their life – make a **pilgrimage** to the holy city of Mecca in Saudi Arabia. This seemed a good time for several reasons. Muslim

▲ Malcolm with boxer Cassius Clay (later Muhammad Ali) in March 1964. They had just watched a screening of Clay's victory over Sonny Liston.

Mosque, Inc. was up and running, and the continuing threats to his life made it advisable for him to spend some time abroad. Most important of all, it seems likely he needed to strengthen his faith and sense of purpose after the split with Elijah Muhammad, who had been like a second father to him.

Money was a problem. Malcolm had never earned more than expenses from the Nation of Islam, and such a trip would cost a great deal. But, as often in his life, his sister Ella was willing to help him out. In mid-April he was able to leave for the Middle East.

## Mecca

The five-week trip proved a wonderful experience. His flight to Egypt included a stopover in Frankfurt, and Malcolm was amazed at how friendly the Germans were towards him. In Cairo he joined a group of pilgrims bound for Mecca, and was struck by how little skin colour seemed to matter. He felt, he wrote later, as if he had just 'stepped out of a prison'. On the flight to Jeddah, the last stop before Mecca, he was invited to meet the captain, whose skin was several shades darker than his own: 'I had never seen a black man flying a jet,' he wrote.

Only followers of **Islam** are allowed into the site of pilgrimage in Mecca, and Malcolm was held up in Jeddah while the authorities checked his Islamic **credentials**. The Nation of Islam was not considered truly Islamic, but Arab friends – men who would, Malcolm knew, have been considered white in America – happily vouched for him and offered him hospitality. That morning, he said, was 'the start of a radical alteration in my whole outlook about "white" men'.

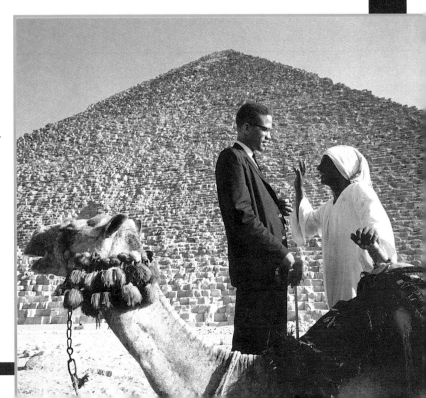

▶ *Malcolm in Egypt in 1964. He met many different people on the trip, which changed his perception of who were his enemies and who were his supporters.*

In Mecca he joined thousands of others in circling the sacred black stone Ka'aba and performing all the other age-old **rituals**. There was, he said, a 'spirit of unity and brotherhood that my experiences in America had led me to believe never could exist between the white and the non-white.' He wrote to Betty and his colleagues at Muslim Mosque, Inc., telling them of his experiences, and of how they had changed his attitudes. He signed the letters with a new name, El-Hajj Malik El-Shabazz.

## Green light

*'I was in my car driving ... when at a red light another car pulled alongside. ... next to me, was a white man. "Malcolm X!" he called out – and when I looked, he stuck his hand out of his car, across at me, grinning. "Do you mind shaking hands with a white man?" Imagine that! Just as the traffic light turned green, I told him, "I don't mind shaking hands with human beings. Are you one?"'*
(From *The Autobiography of Malcolm X*)

Although he still thought America was heading for a racial catastrophe, he was newly optimistic about the future. A few years earlier, asked by a white student what she could do to help, he had told her: 'nothing'. Now he was ready to believe that at least some of the younger American whites were capable of understanding the truth about their country, and of acting to help change it.

## The new Malcolm

After he had completed the pilgrimage, Malcolm spent several weeks touring the Middle East and Africa. In country after country he hammered home his old message of African American suffering, but he was now also stressing the need for a link-up between African Americans and Africa. Such a political alliance, he believed, would give both sides more clout in their dealings with the white-ruled world.

Back in America, he told a huge array of journalists that he no longer believed all white men were evil: 'I know now,' he said, 'that some white people are truly sincere, that some truly are capable of being brotherly toward a black man.' He also made it very clear that he was as angry as ever about the African American situation, and had no intention of reducing his attacks on the government. On the contrary, he was considering charging the USA with 'denial of **human rights**' at the United Nations. The more perceptive journalists were left wondering whether this new Malcolm, with his more balanced views and wider appeal, might be even more dangerous than the old one.

# 10

# Marked for death

Through the years of his marriage Malcolm had often been an absent husband and father. Betty later said that 'when he was home the whole house was happy', that the quality of the family's time together made up for the amount of time he spent away, but Malcolm himself was not so sure. In 1964 he told Alex Haley, the writer who was helping him with his autobiography, that he had never bought a present for any of his children. 'That's not good, I know it,' he said. 'I've always been too busy.'

When he was at home the family would sometimes go to the beach together, and Malcolm would work on his speeches while Betty played or swam with the children. He read poetry to them, and was, according to Betty, 'very good at it'. She

remembered times when Malcolm was watching himself on television – the children would go up to the screen to take a closer look and then come back and check that it was their father sitting in the chair beside them.

When he was going to be away for a while he used to leave love letters and small sums of money hidden around their New York house, and then telephone telling Betty where to look for them.

◀ *A photograph of Malcolm X taken in March 1964.*

## Last months

On 28 June 1964, he announced the founding of the
Organization of Afro-American Unity, which aimed to
represent the interests of all people of African descent,
whether in Africa itself or the Americas. A few days after this
he was on his way back to Africa, this time for a tour of
eleven countries which lasted almost five months. He spoke at
the Organization of African Unity summit in Cairo; all across
the continent he talked to African heads of state and
addressed meetings and conferences. Everywhere he went he
told audiences that Africans and **African Americans** would
be stronger if they stood together.

He came home in November to the birth of a fourth
daughter, Gamilah, and more death threats. At first he felt
certain the **Nation of Islam** was behind these threats, but
then, as he told Alex Haley, he began to doubt this. He started
wondering whether some government agency was trying to
kill him. Either way, the word on the streets of Harlem was
that Malcolm was 'marked for death'. Now, in public, he
surrounded himself with **Muslim** Mosque, Inc. bodyguards.

## The same old story

*'Our position has never changed. If you sit at the back of the
plane and it's going a hundred miles an hour, and you're on the
back of the plane, well, it can start going a thousand miles an
hour; you're going faster, but you're still at the back of the
plane. And that's the way it is with the Negro in this society –
we started out at the rear and we're still at the rear.'*

(Malcolm X, in an interview with
journalist Claude Lewis, December 1964)

◀ *Malcolm's wife and children. From left to right: Qubilah, Gamilah, Betty, Attalah and Ilyasah.*

At home, in the early hours of 14 February 1965, he and his family were awakened by a huge blast. Someone had thrown two firebombs through their windows. Malcolm and Betty quickly gathered together their terrified children and carried them to safety. Watching the house burn Malcolm must have thought back 35 years to that night in Lansing when his parents had rescued him from a similar fire.

## Death

A week later, on 21 February, Malcolm was scheduled to address an afternoon meeting at Harlem's Audubon Ballroom. He had just started speaking when there was a scuffle a few rows back. 'Let's cool it, brothers,' Malcolm said, but at that moment three men in the front row, two armed with revolvers, one with a shotgun, rose to their feet like a firing squad and opened fire. Malcolm, hit by sixteen bullets and shotgun pellets, was dead before he reached the hospital. He was 39 years old.

Five days later, 22,000 people lined up to view the body, and next morning thousands more stood in the freezing cold to pay their respects. The well-known African American actor Ossie Davis delivered the funeral eulogy: 'Malcolm was our manhood,' he said. 'Our living black manhood! This was his meaning to his people. And, in honouring him, we honour the best in ourselves ... And we will know him then for what he was and is – a Prince – our own black shining Prince! – who didn't hesitate to die, because he loved us so.'

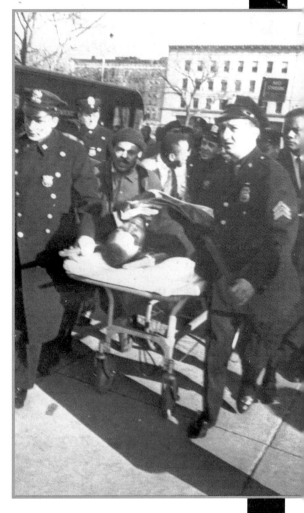

▲ Malcolm's body is taken from the Audubon Ballroom after his fatal shooting, 21 February 1965.

Three men – all Nation of Islam Muslims – were brought to trial. At first they all denied the charge, but then one man both admitted his guilt and swore that the other two had not been there. He said he had been hired, but would not say by whom. All three were found guilty and sentenced to life imprisonment. If they really were hired assassins, the identity of the man or men who hired them remains a mystery.

The years that followed Malcolm's death in February 1965 were the stormiest in post-war American history. Opinions were violently divided over the war in Vietnam, and at times America seemed close to a race war at home. Through the 'long hot summers' of the late 1960s, as city after city erupted in flames, it seemed as if all Malcolm's warnings of a racial catastrophe were coming true. For a few short years **militant** new groups like the Black Panthers, which seemed to reflect much of what Malcolm had stood for, captured the imagination of many young **African Americans**.

Yet groups like the Black Panthers, harassed by the police and uncertain of their strategies, achieved very little. African Americans were left only with the limited gains won by the **civil rights** movement: legal equality and freedom to compete economically. Almost 40 years later African Americans are still far more likely to be poor or unemployed than whites.

## A life cut short

Elijah Muhammad and the **Nation of Islam** gave Malcolm the chance to make use of his immense talents as a politician, but the organization's narrow **separatist** vision – its refusal to imagine any positive relationship between different races – proved, in the end, a stifling experience. Less than a year passed between Malcolm's split with the Nation and his death, but in that time he did move away from separatism and towards a more internationalist point of view. Had he lived, it seems probable he would have further refined his political position: he still had much to learn about the world beyond America.

BLACK HERITAGE

USA
33

MALCOLM X
EL-HAJJ MALIK EL-SHABAZZ

1999

*◀ The US postage stamp issued in honour of Malcolm X, more than a quarter of a century after his death.*

## A lasting voice

Malcolm told the truth about race relations in America. He picked at the **myths** and the half-truths and the wishful thinking until only the bare bones of truth remained. He made many white Americans painfully aware of a past and a present they would rather have ignored; he forced many African Americans to face up to the painful reality of their situation, and to stop pretending that they could cheerfully bear what was actually unbearable. He spoke for the urban poor, for the frustrated young, for all who found themselves banging their heads against the wall of **racial discrimination**.

Malcolm is still speaking for African Americans today. His *Autobiography*, chosen by *Time* magazine as one of the ten most important non-fiction works of the 20th century, is still widely read. His voice can be heard on tapes of his speeches from Harlem to the farthest reaches of Africa.

Historians have emphasized the differences between 'violent' Malcolm and 'non-violent' Martin Luther King, who was also assassinated at the age of 39. But by the end of their lives there was little to separate the beliefs of the two men. Both had concluded that **racism** was too deeply rooted in American society and the American economic system for a quick or easy solution. Although Malcolm always refused to rule out violence in self-defence, he never advocated physical aggression.

## The choice

'There are two kinds of Negroes. ... The house Negro always looked out for his master. ... He loved his master more than his master loved himself. ... If the master got sick, he'd say, "What's the matter, boss, we sick?" When the master's house caught afire, he'd try and put the fire out. He didn't want his master's house burned.
...

'But then you had some field Negroes, who lived in the huts, had nothing to lose. They wore the worst kind of clothes. They ate the worst food. ... They felt the sting of the lash. They hated their master.

'If the master got sick, they'd pray that the master died. If the master's house caught fire, they'd pray for a strong wind to come along. That was the difference between the two.

'And today you still have house Negroes and field Negroes.

'I'm a field Negro.'
   (Malcolm X, speaking in Selma, Alabama, three weeks before his death)

Malcolm was certainly not a violent man himself. On the contrary, the great American writer James Baldwin considered him one of the gentlest people he ever knew. Baldwin once chaired a radio show in which the two guests were Malcolm and a young student. He was afraid that Malcolm would 'simply eat the boy alive', but nothing proved further from the truth. 'Malcolm understood that child,' Baldwin said, 'and talked to him as though he was talking to a younger brother ... What struck me most was that he was not trying to proselytize [convince] the child: he was trying to make him think.'

That was Malcolm X's legacy. He forced Americans of all colours to think about their racial history, their racial present and their racial future – about what it really meant to be human.

▲ A photograph of Malcolm X taken for Life magazine by the famous photographer Eve Arnold.

## A provocative man

'You can imagine what a howling, shocking nuisance this man was to both Negroes and whites. Once Malcolm fastened onto you, you could not escape. ... He would make you angry as hell, but he would also make you proud. It was impossible to remain defensive and apologetic about being a Negro in his presence. He wouldn't let you.'

(African American actor Ossie Davis remembering Malcolm X)

# Timeline

| | |
|---|---|
| 1925 | Malcolm Little born in Omaha (19 May). |
| 1928 | Family buys a house in East Lansing. |
| 1929 | House set on fire by white **racists** (December). |
| 1930 | First **Nation of Islam** temple founded. |
| 1931 | Malcolm's father killed (28 September). |
| 1938 | Fostered out to Gohannas family. |
| 1939 | Mother has complete nervous breakdown. |
| 1941 | Malcolm moves to Boston, takes various jobs. |
| 1942 | Moves to Harlem, New York City. |
| 1945 | Returns to Boston, forms burglary gang. |
| 1946 | Arrested, tried and jailed. |
| 1952 | Released from prison, moves to Detroit (August). First meeting with Elijah Muhammad (September). |
| 1953 | Becomes assistant **minister** of Detroit temple (June). |
| 1954 | Sets up temples in Boston, Philadelphia and New York. |
| 1956 | Meets Betty Sanders (later Betty X). |
| 1957 | Hinton Johnson incident. |
| 1958 | Marries Betty X (January), first daughter Attalah born (November). |
| 1959 | Tours Africa as ambassador of Elijah Muhammad. TV news reports *The Hate That Hate Produced*. |
| 1960 | **African American** student **sit-in** movement begins. Birth of second daughter Qubilah (December). |
| 1962 | Hears rumours of Elijah Muhammad's affairs. Birth of third daughter Ilyasah (July). |
| 1963 | Confronts Elijah Muhammad with rumours (April). March on Washington (28 August). Assassination of President Kennedy (22 November). |

Malcolm gives 'chickens coming home to roost' speech, and is silenced for 90 days by Elijah Muhammad (December).

1964    Announces break with Nation of Islam, forms **Muslim** Mosque Inc. (March).

Makes **pilgrimage** to Mecca and tours Africa (April–May).

Announces founding of Organization of Afro-American Unity (June).

Tours Africa (July–November).

Birth of fourth daughter Gamilah (November).

1965    House firebombed (14 February).

Malcolm shot dead at New York's Audubon Ballroom (21 February).

Birth of twin daughters Malaak and Malikah (autumn).

# Key people of Malcolm X's time

*Marcus Garvey* (1887–1940) was born in Jamaica. He founded the Universal Negro Improvement Association in 1914, which campaigned for **African American civil rights** and **economic independence** from the white community. An eccentric figure who liked wearing flashy uniforms, Garvey invented the slogan 'Black is Beautiful' and encouraged the idea of African Americans returning to Africa. His popularity grew rapidly, but some in the white establishment saw his success as a threat to American national security. Investigations into his business dealings resulted – many thought unfairly – in his imprisonment for fraud. He died in obscurity, but his influence extended into the 1960s with the rise of black power and black **separatism**.

*Lyndon B. Johnson* (1908–73) became vice-president when John F. Kennedy was elected president in 1960. As vice-president, Johnson automatically became president when Kennedy was assassinated in November 1963. He steered Kennedy's second Civil Rights Bill through **Congress** in 1964, and later in the same year defeated Barry Goldwater in the presidential election. In 1965 he forced through the Voting Rights Bill, but his ambitious social programme was undercut by his determination to win the Vietnam War. The growing unpopularity of the war was the main reason for his decision not to stand for re-election in 1968.

*John F. Kennedy* (1917–63) spent fourteen years in Congress before being elected president in November 1960. He supported civil rights for African Americans, but believed that concentration on this one issue would prevent him from achieving anything in other areas he considered just as important. Consequently, his early civil rights measures were half-hearted. He was finally forced to establish civil rights by African American pressure and his awakening conscience. He was assassinated in November 1963, but his Civil Rights Bill became law under his successor Lyndon Johnson.

*Martin Luther King Jr.* (1929–68) sprang to prominence as the leader of the Montgomery Bus Boycott (1955), which many saw as the start of the civil rights movement. A Christian **minister**, he followed the example of India's Mohandas Gandhi in making non-violence the key ingredient of his political campaigns. His campaigns in Birmingham (1963) and Selma (1964) forced Presidents Kennedy and Johnson into adopting far-reaching civil rights and voting rights legislation. He campaigned with equal determination but less success against **economic discrimination** in northern US states and the Vietnam War, and was assassinated in 1968.

*Elijah Muhammad* (born Poole) (1897–1975) grew up in Georgia but moved to Detroit, Michigan in 1923. He was a follower of Marcus Garvey, but when Garvey's movement went into decline he joined Wallace Fard's even more separatist-minded Temple (later **Nation**) **of Islam**. He set up Temple Number Two for Fard in Chicago, and when Fard disappeared in 1934 he assumed leadership of the movement. He corresponded with Malcolm X during the latter's prison years, and through the 1950s came to rely on him more and more. During this period the movement expanded to include schools, restaurants, shops and farms. Elijah fell out with Malcolm X in 1963, and many still believe he was involved in Malcolm's assassination. He died in 1975 and was succeeded by his son Wallace Muhammad.

# Further reading & other resources

## Further reading

*John F. Kennedy*, David Downing, Heinemann Library, 2001

*To Kill a Mockingbird*, Harper Lee, Heinemann, 1960

*Malcolm X*, Walter Dean Myers, Scholastic Inc., 1993

*Malcolm X for Beginners*, Bernard Aquina, Writers & Readers, 1992

*Martin Luther King Jr.*, David Downing, Heinemann Library, 2002

## Sources

*The Autobiography of Malcolm X*, Malcolm X (as told to Alex Haley), Ballantine, 1973 (all quotes not attributed otherwise are from this source)

*Malcolm X, the Man and his Times*, John Henrik Clarke (ed.), Collier, 1969

*Malcolm X as They Knew Him*, David Gallen (ed.), Carroll & Graf, 1992

*A People's History of the United States*, Howard Zinn, Longman, 1996

## Films

*In the Heat of the Night* (directed by Norman Jewison, starring Sidney Poitier and Rod Steiger)

*To Kill A Mockingbird* (directed by Robert Mulligan, starring Gregory Peck)

*Malcolm X* (directed by Spike Lee, starring Denzel Washington)

## Websites

The Autobiography of Malcolm X Teaching Guide: www.randomhouse.com/BB/teachers/tgs/malcolmx.html

Malcolm X: A Research Site: www.brothermalcolm.net/mxcontext.html

# Glossary

**African American** in the USA, American with African ancestors. During Malcolm X's lifetime the words 'coloured', 'negro' and 'black' were also used by this community to describe itself. The words 'nigger', 'darkie' and 'rastus' were commonly used by whites as a racial insult.

**Allah** Muslim name for God

**cat-burglar** burglar who enters buildings by climbing

**civil rights** legal rights of all people to the same equal opportunities and benefits

**confidence trick** scheme for fooling someone into giving up their money

**Congress** law-making arm of the US government, comprising the Senate and the House of Representatives

**conk** in the USA, the process of flattening and straightening hair by applying a burning substance called congolene, popular among African Americans particularly in the 1940s and 1950s

**correspondence course** course of study conducted by post

**cracker** in US, insulting slang term for poor whites

**credentials** evidence of achievements or trustworthiness

**credit** promise of payment at some agreed future date

**economic discrimination** unfair treatment in matters relating to the economy (e.g. work availability, work conditions and pay, housing, education and health care)

**FBI** in the USA, Federal Bureau of Investigation. It investigates crimes to do with internal security.

**federal government** in the USA, the central government based in Washington DC. Federal laws made by the federal government must be observed throughout the USA, and override state laws.

**foster home** home in which a child is brought up by adults who are not his or her own parents

**Great Depression** worldwide period of great economic hardship which began around 1929 and lasted for most of the following decade

**human rights** rights which should belong to any person

**integration** bringing together, breaking down barriers. In racial matters, integration is the opposite of segregation.

**Islam** one of the world's three major monotheistic (one God) religions (along with Christianity and Judaism), founded by the Prophet Muhammad in the 7th century

**juvenile detention home** place where young offenders are held for a short period

**Ku Klux Klan** society of racist whites formed after the American Civil War with the aim of keeping blacks in an inferior position. Famous for its white hoods and burning crosses, it was responsible for hundreds of murders of African Americans. In the 1950s and 1960s it violently opposed the civil rights movement, and survives to this day in various parts of the world.

**life insurance** payments made during a person's lifetime which guarantee a lump sum payment after death for those specified in the policy, usually partners or children of the person

**Midwest** an area in the north central part of the USA

**militant** aggressively active in support of a cause

**minister** clergyman

**Muslim** follower of Islam. In the USA, also used to describe follower of Nation of Islam.

**myth** story which usually uses supernatural or imaginary characters to make a point about how and why people have become the way they are

**Nation of Islam** African American separatist organization founded in the early 1930s by Wallace Fard Muhammad, and subsequently led by Elijah Muhammad. Malcolm X was its chief spokesman between 1958 and 1964.

**numbers game**  in the USA, illegal type of gambling which involves guessing which number will come up

**oppression**  harsh and unjust domination

**philosophy**  the study of ideas about life

**pilgrimage**  journey to a holy place

**probation**  period in which offender risks going to prison if he breaks any of the accompanying rules

**racial discrimination**  treating people badly because they belong to a particular racial group

**racism**  treating individuals or groups differently (and usually worse) merely because they belong to a different race. People who do this are called **racists**.

**reform school**  school for correcting the behaviour of young criminal offenders or law breakers

**rituals**   things repeated the same way, usually at regular intervals and for religious reasons

**segregation**  in racial matters, the enforced separation of races

**separatism**  in the USA, racial matters, separate development and institutions for whites and African Americans, not excluding the possibility of separate countries

**sit-in**  method of protest, involving sitting down and refusing to be moved, which was first widely used against segregated Southern lunch counters in early 1960

**slavery**  ownership of other human beings (called slaves), usually from other ethnic backgrounds

**slave trade**  capture or purchase, transporting and selling of slaves

**the South**  in the USA, usually taken to mean those south-eastern states which made up the Confederate side in the American Civil War

**surveillance**  keeping watch on, usually secretly

**welfare**  in the USA, financial support given to those in need

# Index